NOT ON THE SIDE
OF THE GODS

OTHER TITLES BY ANNA CROWE

Skating Out of the House (Peterloo, 1997)
L'Ànima del teixidor / The weaver's soul
with Stewart Conn (Proa, 2000)
Punk with Dulcimer (Peterloo, 2006)
A Secret History of Rhubarb (Mariscat Press, 2004)
Figure in a Landscape (Mariscat Press, 2010)
Finding my Grandparents in the Peloponnese (Mariscat Press 2013)
Punk con salterio / Punk with Dulcimer,
translated by Joan Margarit (Spain: Cosmopoética, 2008)
Paisatge amb figura / Figure in a Landscape
with lithographs by Andreu Maimó (Mallorca: Ensiola, 2011)
Figura en un paisaje, translated by Pedro Serrano
(Mexico: El oro de los tigres, 2019)

TRANSLATIONS

Light off water / Miralls d'aigua, XXV Catalan poems,
(Carcanet / Scottish Poetry Library, 2007)
Music and Scurvy, poems by Anna Aguilar-Amat
(Catalan / English / Macedonian, Blesok, 2006)
Tugs in the fog, poems by Joan Margarit (Bloodaxe 2006)
Strangely happy, poems by Joan Margarit (Bloodaxe 2011)
Six Catalan Poets, anthology edited by Pere Ballart (Arc, 2013)
Peatlands, poems by Pedro Serrano (Arc, 2014)
Love is a place, poems by Joan Margarit (Bloodaxe, 2016)
Lunarium, poems by Josep-Lluís Aguiló (Arc, 2016)
Maps of Desire poems by Manuel Forcano (Arc, 2019)

NOT ON THE SIDE OF THE GODS

ANNA CROWE

Arc
PUBLICATIONS
2019

Published by Arc Publications,
Nanholme Mill, Shaw Wood Road
Todmorden OL14 6DA, UK
www.arcpublications.co.uk

978 1911469 91 9 (pbk)
978 1911469 92 6 (hbk)

Design by Tony Ward

Cover picture:
'Raven' by Pat Bray
by kind permission of the artist.

Editor for the UK & Ireland
John Wedgewood Clarke

AUTHOR'S ACKNOWLEDGEMENTS

Some of the poems in this collection first appeared in *Artemis* (Second Light), *The Café Review* (Portland Maine), *The Dark Horse, The Hand that Sees, The High Window, Journal of St Andrews Botanic Garden, Look up Edinburgh* (Freight Books, 2014), *Modern Poetry in Translation, New Writing Scotland, Oversteps Press, The Poetry Paper* (The Poetry Trust, Aldeburgh), *Poetry Scotland, Poetry Spotlight. com, Preserved: Between the Image and the Word* (StAnza exhibition, 2016), *The Rialto, A Secret History of Rhubarb* (Mariscat Press 2004), *The Scores, Sou'wester* (University of South Illinois), *Snakeskin, The Stinging Fly, Surgeons' Hall, a Museum Anthology, Territories* (Scottish Poetry Library and Edinburgh International Book Festival 2014, *There's a Song to be Made*, a 70th birthday tribute to Stewart Conn, 2006; *La Traductière* (www.festrad.com), *The Undertow, Watching Sunlight, Writing Motherhood* (Seren, 2017).

'From the Hinterland' was commissioned by The Royal College of Surgeons, Edinburgh to commemorate their five-hundredth anniversary in 2005; 'Swallows' was commissioned by Shore Poets as the Mark Ogle Memorial Poem.

I am indebted to the composer, Jean-Christopher Rosaz, for setting 'Sephardic Orange Cake' to music for voice and violin, and to Marcus Rees-Roberts, for making a short film based on the same poem.

'Acnestis' was a prize-winner in the Dumfries and Galloway/Wigtown Poetry Competition, 2006; 'Water-Wheels' was a prize-winner in the Autumn Voices poetry competition, 2018; 'The Gecko' won the 2018 Elmet Prize.

My warm thanks go to my friend, the poet Peter Jarvis, and to my colleagues in the Wee Crit Group for all their valuable advice and criticism.

And warmest thanks to my husband, Dr Julian Crowe, my best critic.

ACKNOWLEDGEMENTS

for my grandchildren –
Nayana, Arthur, Imogen,
Alexander, Amanthi

"There's something in me that insists it sings
Freely, for nothing, the lovely, lonely art
Called poetry, an art you understand."

DOUGLAS DUNN
'Venezuela', *The Year's Afternoon*

"Hear it now, see me now
    everything is racing
        everything is vanishing

Love each other, love each other
    everything is hosted
        everything is vanishing

ALEXANDER HUTCHISON
'Everything', *Bones & Breath*

CONTENTS

THE GECKO

in memory of my sister, Rosy

Behind the closed door of the sitting-room
the television blares the stored heat
of the day, and our parents' traded venom
feels its way like a plant towards us
where we stand on the dark stairs.
This will be our final conversation.

While you talk, voice cracking with strain,
I stare at a tiny gecko splayed
against the window. How have you clung
so long to the slippery pane of glass
that is the family? Flesh-coloured,
almost transparent in the naked

glare of the bulb in its wrought-
iron cradle blotted by moths,
the gecko is motionless –
but for the tongue, fast-forwarding
towards death; a flicker
each time I almost miss,

intent on your catalogue of grief.
I hear how you're racked,
caught between love and duty, taut
and sickening in that atmosphere.
– *I must hang on*, low and fierce.
I have to hold it together.

I stare at the lidless eyes, the delicate
feet; its toes like tiny spoons
pressed flat against the window.
The gecko, says my book, adheres

13

to a vertical plane by means
of minute platelets armed with hairs.

But how did you stick to that joyless
touting of timeshares – your smile
embracing *the ample storage space*
where all your words would soon be lost?
You may have thought you could lessen
the pressure of debt (the pain in your chest

we're about to learn is a clot on the lung), but
– *I think I'm losing my husband,* you whisper.
I turn to look at you, and you're weeping.
And when I look back, the gecko is gone.

BASSEY
Equus ferus caballus

You barely see him in this huge assemblage
of bones joined by wires and propped up on
an elegant cast-iron frame: a skeleton
of bleached spars and spavined thwarts, ribcage
a foundered barrel of staves, he stands wrecked
on the long reef of his spine. The breastbone –
that took the strain of hauling quarried stone
to the mason's yard to be cut then trekked
to Arbroath's pier – is grey, threadbare homespun.
On tiptoe you can peer right through his sight-
less orbits all the way to the vertebrae
of the great neck that rippled in the sun,
that Robert Stevenson would slap, and say,
This is the horse that built the Bell Rock Light.

Note: Bassey the carthorse pulled 2,000 tonnes of stone, between
1807 and 1811, from quarry to mason's yard and thence to the pier in
Arbroath, to be ferried out at low tide to build the first existing rock
lighthouse in the British Isles on the notorious Inchcape Reef. Put out
to grass on Inchkeith in the Forth, Bassey died in 1818. His skeleton
was bought, prepared and displayed by the anatomist Dr John Barclay,
and was later gifted to the Royal College of Surgeons in Edinburgh,
before being transferred to the Bell-Pettigrew Museum in St Andrews
in 1922. Bassey was also commemorated by Robert Stevenson, who
named one section of the Bell Rock in honour of the horse. The model
lighthouse above the porch of the offices of the Northern Lighthouses
Board is a replica of the Bell Rock lighthouse.

15

PASSING WEATHER

for Anne Stevenson

"And what's 'to make'?

To be and to become words' passing
weather;"

ANNE STEVENSON, 'Making Poetry', *The Fiction-Makers*

You hear their voices at the edge
    of sleep, birds calling from forest or coast,
and sense they are waiting

for a signal, a shift of weather or
    light like a bright clearing, a bell-buoy's
clang, that will bring them tilting

and swerving, composing
    an eye, a comma, a pupa, a leaf,
in close-up or distant,

a dark murmuration that finds
    you and fills your ears and eyes
and pulls you in to ride

the storm of the poem with them until
    they have shaped themselves to the sound,
the being they want, and drop you.

NIGHT OF THE FECUNDATION OF THE TREES

"If the Kalends, or first of January, falls on the moon's day, Monday, then there will be a severe and confused winter"
COTTON TIBERIUS A.iii (Anglo-Saxon manuscript in British Library)

"The first night of the New Year, when the wind blows from the west, they call dàr-na-coille in the Gaelic tongue, the 'night of the fecundation of the trees'."
JOHN SINCLAIR *Statistical History of Scotland*, 1794

2 a.m. The wind has risen and woken me.
I lie and listen to its voice, feeling the house
shuddering, down at its roots. What's that word?
Sough: the wind and the conifers are soughing,
and you beside me, breathing deeply, sighing.

Yesterday was New Year's Day, and a Monday.
I think of our stripling apple trees:
Arthur Turner, 'having the finest blossom
of any variety'; *James Grieve*, mild and sweet,
the 'paragon of Scottish Victorian apples'.
They came with the snow, and now are heeled-in merely,
dormant under the frost in the iron-hard garden.

Saxons, Gaels, orangepippintrees.com,
we pray the wind that rocks our apple-lads
won't wake them from their winter sleep
until the earth relents and we can plant them,
each one upright to salute the spring.

17

HOW TO FORETELL THE ARRIVAL OF SPRING

for Robyn Marsack

by the blackthorn's hailstone flowers unfurling

by the owl who calls down dusk – softly softly
or the blackbird's meltwater song, at four in the morning

by the nervous bouncing of gnats above the burn
and winter heliotrope's stealthy waft
of lemon-vanilla along the braes

by the ray of sun on the Feast of the Annunciation
piercing at noon a round window in the south wall
of the nave of Pisa's *Duomo* to kindle a marble egg
that sits on its small ledge by Giovanni Pisano's pulpit

by turning Ilke's old *Season Coffee* canister on the shelf
ninety degrees clockwise to cancel the snow-face and reveal
a farm and the green meadows of rural Luxembourg
where newly-arrived swallows perch on a fence to confer –
home-lovers whose twittering fills your kitchen

THE SWALLOWS' NEST

for Hugh and Jo

At Huntly, windows innocent
of glass, the lord's hall
stands open to every weather.
Hard to remember
such places once were home –
so eloquent of war
and the ruin war brings
their ruined walls are –
but for the swallows
swooping in through the windows
or up the winding stair
to build their bee-skep nests
on every wall: beakful after
beakful of patient mud
the colour of honey.
The air parts, and a bird
swims on its own whistling cry
into the huge cold fireplace
to vanish behind the chimney-breast.
Imagine the young emerging,
seeing by day
a bright blue eye; later,
crepuscular through sooty down,
a sparkling star.

COMMON RUSH

for Swithun

The flowers, by August, brownish withered knots;
but something about the way they sprout –

growing so far, no further, up the stem
as though to exemplify the golden mean,

while the smooth shaft carries on
to its fine conclusion –

brings you to mind: balance, a willingness
to live within your strength, content with less.

Climbing Massanella, under your grandfather's taunts
you shrank into a stubborn, reed-like patience—

thin adolescent who'd outgrown his strength—
choosing to stay beside the cave's mouth.

When we came down hours later,
you showed me the spring and chained cup: water

brimmed a rocky basin, before spilling over
into the dark. On the summit, black vultures

had been mere specks. Leaving
the cave, you pointed at what I'd missed: thriving

tucked between a step's riser and tread,
cyclamen balearicum; rare, sweet-scented.

THE FIELD OF THE WRITING

Achadh Scriobach, Co Tyrone, literally 'Field of the Writing,'
whose name derives from the stone with its Ogham inscription:
'Dotetto Maqi Maglani', or 'Dotetto Son of Mullen'.

A late sonata brings it back:
trudging like great angels
these double chords walk you
out of a brown tangle of thorns.
Slow sequences of ice
relent in rain; hawthorn
will sweeten into leaf, music
rinse a name on stone.

His fugue had proliferated
    into that web of small back roads
        where you would lose yourself
were it not for the hills running alongside
    emerging into a line
        of rain-washed clarity.
Stone-deaf now, he could not,
    never did hear
        these variations spilling
their fractals of tender larch
    and freckled elder.
        Angled thorns and clouds of sloe
usher us along the small side road,
    into another time, following
        in the imagined steps of mourners.
His variations gather up
    every weather of grief,
        from tinnitus roaring
against an indifferent heaven,
    to anguish shrinking into
        hailstone-numbness;

into a silence brimful
    of remembered birdsong.
        Bearing the lad's body,
the small procession stumbles with bowed heads,
    passing boundaries of elder-tree, burn,
        standing stone, blackthorn:

  here they will set the slab with his name.

        For now we have only the music:
        birdsong holding its own
        with the steady drip of rain;
        rain and bird trilling as one
        as they sing themselves
        into a silence that holds
        all that has gone before,
        all that's to come.

THE FLOWERS OF THE BURREN

for the hibakusha

Here on the Burren, small-leaved cotoneaster
spreads out clouds of flowers upon the rocks;
in Dublin, Merrion Square, your cherry tree
had wept its petals into a fall of snow –
the cherry, first tree to bloom in what was left
of Hiroshima, Nagasaki: "Never
take your eyes off Hiroshima," you wrote,
and in this limestone landscape – pavement fissured
with deep darks like an old grainy photo –
I think of the ones who, in that clap of light,
left only shadows etched into the street.
Vaporised where they stood, they were the lucky
ones who did not live to see the worst
that fire and blast can do to lovely flesh:
the cancers patiently proliferating
out of the poisoned bones of the very young:
these were your witness and your legacy.
And so for you, under a sky no plane
has crossed all week, I name the Burren flowers
your flowers. What looks like barren rock will prove
these grassy terraces of peace, turloughs
of the mind, where you will find the bloody
cranesbill, lady's tresses, lady's mantle,
bitter vetchling and the white burnet-rose;
blue spring-gentians, mountain avens, mountain-
everlasting.

LARKSONG
Alauda arvensis

Afterwards, all he could remember
as he went about the tasks they set him
was the lark winding itself

skywards on its own flight-song,
a pure perpendicular ascent
of implacable sound and fluttering wings

that pinned him where he stood
blinded and deafened to receive
the outpouring like a chrism

or sentence – silence at last
propelling him home, where he found
no face or any thing he had once known.

KNITTING THE GALLARUS ORATORY

for Di Gilpin and Alice Bullough

In grey-brown wool, on four needles,
> the gansey grows, grows heavy:
cables twist on the yoke's panels,
> with ladders, and cobbles of double-moss.
Through the open window, a drift
> of summer phlox, a tang of salt
on a wind from the west that rushes in
> and fills the room with sea-light;
that same wind blows from *An Araglán*
> up the rough road from Dingle Bay,
and my stitches are a net for the sea.
> The rows turn tasselled fuchsia-hedge,
the shoulder-seam a roof-ridge,

> and I'm knitting the Gallarus Oratory,
upturned *curragh* of drystone walls
> where Norah Gorman steps in from the rain,
spreads out her plaid and rests a while
> though her fingers never stop. She knits
the long road to Dublin, her cares
> catching on yarn like burrs on her skirt:
will John, her brother, stay warm
> in Norah's gansey while tunnelling
through Yorkshire rock, building a road
> for that newfangled thing, the railway?
She prays he'll keep dry in the oiled wool
> from Smerwick ewes running through my hands.

John Gorman was probably the name of my great-grandfather, and I
have invented a sister for him.

25

A KILRONAN LULLABY

for Alexander Dashiell Benjamin, b. 23 April 2012

The cuckoo I heard calling a minute ago
has swooped to rest on a dry-stone wall, rocking
and raising its long tail. But never fret:
the meadow-pipit's nest is hidden
deep among rushes where the boreen begins.

I've sewn you a quilt of tiny fields, feather-
stitched with birdsong; the wren peeps through
and then the linnet: gaps between stones are full
of airs; blackbird on the gable-end
pipes the day to a close. Are you asleep?

An Crugán, Kilronan, Inis Mor, May 2012

THE SPACES IN BETWEEN

i. m. Victor Pasmore

The first haar of spring has hidden the Eden
and its estuary: as I round the bend,
the paper-mill trembles into view,
its square mass, chimney, and roof of slanted lights
dissolving in a blur of geometry
that is pure Pasmore; triangles,
cylinder, cube, pink and cygnet grey,
floating above banks of vapour.
As though his *quiet river* had drifted north,
or dawn had dipped its brush in Thames
waters at Pangbourne, say, or Wallingford,
to paint Guardbridge in watercolour.

Later, it was the spaces in between
possessed him: all the solid negatives
that Corfu's searing light bequeaths:
gaps between stones
in dry-stone walls; dark rooms
among the cedar's branches;
the structured nothingness that is not
nothing and demands we name it.

He would have liked this northern haar,
called it a *sea-fret*, applauded
the way it sets things adrift,
estranging the familiar, prompting
memory's dislocations: spaces between
the here and now in which to gather
the swan killed on the bridge,
and the child on his blue tricycle
who pedalled into the Eden;
their memory surfacing this morning
as the kingfisher who rises glittering
through swansdown banks of vapour.

27

AMNIOTIC

for Christopher

Far out in childhood's blue bay
the mast of the *John Eagan Layne*
leaned like a pen in an inkwell;

in summer the willow-pattern china
on the black, worm-eaten welsh dresser
shrugged off light dealt by the sea.

Months before you were born
you were already trying to hurl yourself
free of the water like a salmon,

and in the old Delft-tiled bathroom –
Edwardian country-house turned hospital –
seven months gone, I lay and watched

a wherry's sails waver
in warm water, as children skated,
bowled hoops and played at hopscotch.

While women drew water from a well, or churned
butter, their men-folk fished from dykes, walked
on stilts or followed a plough;

keeping time with ancient plumbing,
windmills on either hand creaked and juddered
and my belly rose above the water

like a small polder. With so much
dedicated labour all around,
I almost believed that when you surfaced

you'd bring my childhood wreck
bubbling up from the sea-bed,
and that the old dresser would rise

with its load of dripping delft. But
by then you were already intent
on your next project, of fathoming the world.

JEWELLER IN THE GALERIE ÉLECTRA, PARIS

Under glass
as though in cabinets of curiosities
dung-beetles, crickets, mantises, bees and ants
all swarm perfectly at home
in Fabre's drawings and notebooks.

Meanwhile
a caddisfly's live, ingenious larva
is building a shelter in a tank of water;
the insect makes its calm selection
from a heap of curated materials
taking them as chance supplies them;
it tweaks fragments into place
with bristly forelegs, binding them
with sticky threads of its secreted silk
into a tubular travelling house.

This is built, not from reed straws
or the empty shells of pond-snails
(from which it made a splendid patchwork scabbard),
but motes of gold and flakes of turquoise
and carnelian, freshwater pearls, fashioning
in its innocence a jewelled refuge.

Note. Jean Henri Fabre, 1823-1915, is considered by many to be the
father of modern entomology, pioneering the close observation
of living creatures in their natural habitat. Much of his enduring
popularity is due to his marvellous teaching ability and his manner
of writing about the lives of insects in biographical form.

SEA-SILK

in homage to Jen Hadfield

So fine, a pair of gloves would fit
inside a snuff-box, a pair of stockings
in half a walnut shell.

In the *Shuyiji* – 'Accounts of Marvels' –
it's claimed this mermaid-silk was woven
by the Kău, the dragon-people,

famed for their skill at the loom;
believed to dwell in water like fish
it was said their eyes could weep pearls.

It's the pen-shell that exudes this silk,
gluing itself to rock and making a home
amongst the world's dwindling seagrass.

POEM

after Banks' Oar-Fish / Regalecus Banksii

Impelled to the surface
by who knows
what grim upheaval
down there in the dark,
she swims to us
through a tangle
of fishermen's tales
to cast herself ashore
on the quiet coasts
of remote islands.
Few folk ever see her,
yet her monstrous length
is the clattered talk
of the ocean-going albatross,
the mournful complaint
of the great northern loon,
the grey seal's moan.
We can only dream
of her skin of smooth silver,
her long, long back
pricked out with fins
like crimson flames.
For now, all we have
is this painted cast
of her small neat head,
her shining, sightless eyes.

ARAN STITCHES

You'd think it barren, this lavender-grey rock.
But then up close, deep in mossy pockets,
you find cowslips, fragrant

orchids, bloody cranesbill,
blue-eyed gentians, thyme
and roseroot, maidenhair fern.

Rock become works of art,
labour of the back-broken centuries;
enclosing their cloak-of-patches fields,

these dry-stone walls are slabs
laid slantwise, tilted left then right;
set like fishnet, or herringbone;

patterns a fisherman's wife
would work for her man's gansey –
love's fingerprint in yarn – *fishtail*

and *lantern* for Pádraic; *twisted cable*
and *hourglass* for Colm. Against the day
the sea might return a body;

so there might be no doubt: the face
gone, a man's shell could drift home
with *waves*, and *hearts*, and *scallops*;

home to *moss*, and *bramble*, and *fern*,
making landfall in the arms
of *tree-of-life*; of *honeycomb*.

THE FENNEL ANNUNCIATION

i. m. Ellen Graves

I have come like a pilgrim
home, pulled up the blind
on the cold back garden and seen,
among late lilies and neglected roses,
the fennel grown to a tree of light:
its sheathed stems, hung with rain,
offer with glittering arms
seedheads like open palms,
like constellations.

Lingering in Gabriel's chapel
and ringed with that bright company
my eyes had combed the vaulting
that fans out high in Bell Harry.
But the fennel's architecture
builds then dwells in its own space
unaware of its green-gold beauty –
archangel in our flower-bed,
shivering as it reads the wind.

SEPHARDIC ORANGE CAKE

for Andreu Maimó

Take 2 oranges. It's an act

of faith, imagination, memory:

walk in our fathers' orchards at Montuïri

and claim the golden fruit there. Take it back.

Boil then crush to a pulp. Light the oven

feeding almond shells into the flames.

Almond, the first flowers of the year, that came

as hope comes to the exile, sharp, unbidden.

Beat together eggs and honey, beat

until combined in forced conversions, lands

in Lluc, in Inqua, Petra, Biniaraix,

all seized, resistance crushed. *Fold fruit, ground almonds,*

into mixture; bake for centuries. Eat

and remember why such sweetness tastes of ash.

KEYS

i. m. Janka Blatt

'Denn wir sind nur die Schale und das Blatt'
(Then we are no more than bark and leaf)
RAINER MARIA RILKE

Bunches of keys
hanging from the dying ash
near your old house
remind me of you
and of your final months:
how you were forever
mislaying your house-keys,
getting them confused,
holding them up to us, upset
and baffled, you with degrees
in psychology and economics.
As though the refugee you'd been
doubted you had truly escaped
and that here was home,
and feared these same keys,
worn and once familiar,
might unlock another door
and you might suddenly step –
like the beloved aunt
who had sent you into safety –
over the threshold
of Auschwitz.

A DREAM OF LOCHORE MEADOWS

i. m. Maurice Taylor OBE,
former Chief Planning Officer of Fife Regional Council

for pit-bings   small green hills

for the old pits' toxic meres   clear lochans   waterbirds   fish

for slag and slurry   flower meadows   birchwoods   birdsong

for coal-dust   selfheal   eyebright   butterfly orchids

nine years of dangerous work
of bulldozers chained together for safety

creeping their way round six pits
some as deep as hell   some still burning

gold catching the light like flame
he turns the medal in his hand   lingers

shamefaced on his adamant caveat
I'll accept it only if Sandy gets one as well

seeing again the man in the leading cab
high on Benarty's black hill   and tiny

leading his team of diggers to level the slag
ploughing it down   sowing rigs of fire

WATER-WHEELS

Straddling the entire breadth
of the stream, we turn

powering no machinery now –
no cloth for fulling

no dyeing-vats to stir
(tainting the brook

where now its pebbles shine) –
but letting the clear-eyed Sorgue

push down each paddle
to send the great wheel

clattering round for nothing
but the sheer pleasure

of moving to water's rhythm.
We are like women

whose children have left home:
skirts kilted, paddling

we're in our element,
tasting our mother-tongue.

Carriero di Tenchurié, Avignon

HOMING

Somewhere in the Borders,
they start to overtake us: lorries heading south
weaving easily in and out of the fast lane
with their freight – a feather-weight
of racing-pigeons.

As the big transporter hurtles past,
carrying them ever further from home,
imagine each bird – eyes closed,
quiet in the hampered dark –
hearing, above

the slap and whine of canvas,
the siren-song of the power-lines;
the miles unspooling beneath the wheels
into a line of music the mind will tag
with accidentals.

Hills like a drag of darkness,
and that quick tug on the line that says
river; cities and towns like interference,
a twitter of static they'll be released into.
Freed, clocked-out

in ceremonies they patiently endure.
Imagine them soaring then, slipping
a sleeve of air to catch the pull of earth,
attuned to memory's pulse,
to frequencies

of starlight. As they listen in to the firths
with their point and counterpoint –
the lighthouses singing, the bridges – small towns
begin to make sense, and forests breathe out
familiar air.

That clock-face with its tower is known;
that gable-end; this garden drenched with night
and its November smell of bonfires
and creosote, and rain on the sprouts
lighting them home.

WASP-BYKE

Three times they have come to build
in a house like a woman's ageing body,
its rooms emptied of children,
their jars of shells and agates
left like stretch-marks,
dusty books like scar tissue.
Behind our bedroom wall
the wasps smelled out
this numb crevice the body forgot.

A motor revved at dawn
or sea far-off or fridge-song
by night had fanned to furnace-strength.
When I put my ear to the wall
the sound burned like shock.
Not anaphylaxis' torpor and chill
but rage, desire, dangerous life.
When I rapped with my knuckles
the clamour rose like fever
until I thought they'd come
bursting through lath and plaster
into the room. We had them poisoned.

In the silence I go on hearing them,
telling myself it's the sea,
the beginnings of tinnitus.
But this is a haunting, a memory
from when my body sang
like a taut string,
alive: when you
had only to lay your hand
in love upon my skin,
and I burned.

MIRAGE IN THE BOTANICAL GARDEN
Rhododendron fastigiatus

Some plants are all dazzle and shriek.
Queening it in the tropical house,
Strelitzia thrusts its bird-of-paradise beak
and spiky, yellow-flame mohican
out of a clutch of sword-like leaves
like a courtesan snapping open her fan.

Others are more subtle. Beyond the pond,
a smoky purple hovers, seeping in
through twigs of a low spreading evergreen;
then, up close, the colour's gone;
no flowers yet, just tiny shoots, conical,
creamy yellow. Try retreating, keeping
half an eye on things, until the mystery
is re-enacted, whatever it may be

.

THE CLOSING RING

Coral atoll, hawksbill turtle's

prized, seductive shell,

osprey's broad patrolling circles,

ringed plover, collared dove,

skylark's spiraling ascent,

scops owl's fluted single note,

scarlet ring around Sardinian warbler's eye,

garden blackbird's, ringed with gold:

all are shrinking, closing,

vanishing

into the white space

at the heart of the corn cockle flower

already absent from our cornfields

when I was a child.

ACNESTIS

for Joan and Mariona Margarit

There's next-door's cat, trying to reach the word
for the place on the back of its neck the tongue won't stretch to –
does it deserve a name? So much makes do
without: the moment when the last bird
of the species somewhere pours out its song unheard;
there should be a word for the way those mountain shadows
solid with sunset rain rebuilt your house
with a tower, long pulled down; and surely a word
exists for the eye searching a wall again
and again for the window west, now gone; for children
whom a string of butchered larks and wrens
will pierce forever? A thrush sings in the rain
and asks, in gaps between the phrases, why
we have no word for a father or mother whose child dies.

SKYE HAYFIELD

for Margaret and Roger Squires, in memory of David

From the breakfast table, sun pouring in,

I look across at the half-mown lower field:

lines of scythed hay and gathered stooks

like flames; a dark belt of woods, blue ocean,

then the hills of Rum, lavender, clear.

A roofless croft is tucked between two fields;

its gables lift their chimneys like empty hands

as though to wind an ancient skein of smoke

into a path across a field: it's there

for anyone to step through squeaky stubble

and hear a blackbird sing from out

an elder bush, or stand and smell the sea.

I hear it, smell it, sitting here, although

your postcard, propped up on my shelf, chides me

with its field half-mown, and the propped stooks

in that low light cast shadows long as knives.

BEAUTIFUL DEMOISELLE, SANNA BAY

i. m. Alasdair Maclean, who wrote Night Falls on Ardnamurchan

Cut into glistening slabs – his back
a torment, his head a cloud of midges –
peat burned in the crofter's hearth
for maybe two hundred years – a blink
in the eye of a pool where the peat-hag
has filled with rain: eight thousand years
in the making as sphagnum moss decayed,
taking its time, the peat is almost gone;
on moorland plumed with bog-cotton,
the pools gleam with an oily film of blue.

Just so, that underwater dragon,
the nymph of a damselfly, stalks
the burn's bed for a whole year
before it climbs out, shucks its skin,
and flies on wings of blue-black silk.
Pinned like an emerald brooch
to a blade of yellow flag, here
where the Allt na Sanna flows through
dune-slack, green turf, orchids, it will mate
and die before the summer ends.

46

THE RINGS OF ARDNAMURCHAN

for Pete and Marg Jarvis

I

Why must some things be made small
before we can see them? Think of
Ardnamurchan's volcanic ring-dyke
with its crater, an amphitheatre
where the township of Achnaha
huddles like a lark on her nest.
The ridge has endured the weathering
of millions of years, yet it's hard
to see the whole thing from the ground.
Only when you open up the OS map
do you see those wrinkled contours,
feel their ancient vastness ring you round.

II

When they lifted the tumble of stones –
long thought to be clearance from a field –
and dug in the turf above Swordle Bay
they found the teeth and arm-bone
of a Viking, buried with all his weapons:

>   *spear*
>   *axe*
>   *knife*
>   *shield*
>   *sword (hilt inlaid with silver wire)*
>   *Irish ring-pin*
>   *whetstone from Norway*
>   *drinking-horn*

47

all in a ring of some 200 rivets,
visible presence of the vanished boat.

III

The lens of the telescope in the hide brings you
into the world of three seals off Garbh Eilean
cavorting in the long light of midsummer;
in the waters of Loch Sunart
the fourth, fifth, sixth and seventh rings
are made by the otter no one sees.

EAR BONES OF THE RIGHT WHALE
Balaena mysticetus

after a piece in porcelain by Kyra Clegg

A whaler's souvenir, these bullae
are a pair of purses whose density
protects the delicate ear-bones
tucked inside, as the whale
slams its way up from deep water
through a thick lid of Arctic ice.

In life, the ear-bones are attuned
to the wheezy sighs, explosive riffs
and whistles of whale-kind; the yawns, clicks,
and buzzing fricatives of conversation; those
phrases skittering like a door creaking open
on rooms in a house we've yet to understand.

THE DAY AFTER THE CRASH

we're glad to trail along these quiet lanes
and find St Peter's, North Barningham –

'redundant', vast, built when wool was gold.
Obedient, mindful of birds, we close the door.

Granaried silence. Yesterday's din recedes
inside our heads, settles, and is received

into this dust-mote barn of storied air.
Gashed and broken metal, shock, surrender

to pink-washed walls, to windows' tracery –
their branching stems of stone still flowering

with hops in the hedge, campions in grass;
October sun leans in through clear glass

to burnish a brass knight and his lady:
mediaeval Palgraves, she holds a rosary;

a line of seven children pray for their souls.
In pleated cap and ruff of goffered marble

Sir Austin Palgrave and wife with firm expression
kneel on the other side of the Reformation.

A wealth of folk with their rich flocks, all gone;
now, only two people live in North Barningham.

The wheel-head cross in the floor, a mystery
in brick and flint, is given a further twist

outside, overhead, where a red kite wheels,
scanning, then dismissing us from its fields.

A MOMENT OF CALM

after Max Ernst

It is that particular time of day in the garden:
     clouds bundling up their crumpled linen,
the sun going down golden, somewhere out of sight,
     and the moon rising, huge and pale as a lump of suet.
The conifers are combing the last of the light,
     tips of branches so precisely etched, black and viridian
against a rose-blue dove-grey lemon sky,
     they might be illustrations of fractal geometry.

Birds of day deliver their last electric statements.
     Before the night-owls quit their tenements
and the bottle-green, splintery shindig starts,
     there is only the wind gusting in small sighs,
then a ground-bass you recognise
     as the jumpy percussion of your heart.

AUBADE

for Stewart Conn on his seventieth birthday

This morning the sun has hung not one but two
rainbows over the loch, turning water
from beaten pewter to airiest harebell blue,
and the Tarbert ferry glides like a swan or snowy
birthday-cake across the Minch. In Uig
all candles will be lit as the vessel enters
port, but now there's a great coming and going
of islands: on the horizon, the hills of Harris
hover like old poets swithering whether
to join the ceilidh; they turn on their heel, vanish,
then shimmer back. Yesterday it was snowing,
but now the whitewashed gable-end of a house
on the Kildonan road shines like a just-
starched shirt-front, and even the heather's
wiry kindling glows, winter's grass
rippling from drab to gold on Eilean Mor.
The sun strikes a corrugated roof's rusted
dullness such an almighty blow it roars
redness into the blue, and the buzzard, dazed
with light, floats high above a Pictish loch
as though a huntsman, leaning from the broch,
had loosed his hawk for you this day of days.

BRAIN CORAL
diploria labyrinthiformis

Labyrinth.
A maze of stony folds.
Meanderings on fluted Rosslyn columns
fanning out white: hundreds of tiny polyps
entrenched like sappers, pushing up their ambulacra –
double walls, brochs, barricades, ramparts, frontiers – aragonite
in goffered frills of guipure lace from Limerick or Carrickmacross.
Cheek by jowl, all competing, sending out filaments, tentacles
inching outwards in an underwater Sri Lankan traffic-jam.
Finally conceding they are one organism, they host algae
and sport the long-spined urchin like a diadem.
They become one beautiful, joined-up,
articulate network of generous life;
almost like
a human
brain.

THE MYSTERIOUS STARLING
Aplonis mavornata

'... It seems, just now,
To be happening so very fast;'
       PHILIP LARKIN, 'Going, Going', *High Windows*

... killed while hopping about a tree.
Emptied of song and spirit to a poverty

of feathered skin, *Aplonis mavornata*,
brown and drab, lies in a drawer

in the British Museum, provenance unknown,
for a hundred years. Until Storrs Olson

tracks down a mention in the poet Byron's
uncle's captain's log, with other extinctions:

the bodies of Liholiho and Kamamalu,
king and queen of Hawaii, whom measles blew

away in London, are being shipped
to Honolulu, where their people's lips

part like a wave around the prow
in a great cry. But now

the *Blonde* sails on to touch at Mauke where,
in the space of just two hours,

Bloxham, ship's naturalist, will shoot a pigeon,
kingfisher, starling, as Captain George Anson,

Lord Byron, borrowing one Maria
Graham's notes – scant and drier

than a dead starling – writes: *killed while hopping
about a tree…* The birds were gone, done hopping,

by 1970, when one D.T. Holyoak,
naturalist, returned to Mauke.

1. PARAKEET FLOWER (*Heliconia psittacorum*)

Here is a scarlet parrot
    diving, wings blown back,
feathers a furled, aerodynamic
    overlap: this is the bud,
opening in a steaming hour
    into a golden sunburst
of radiant starfish or, rather,
    dragonflies trailing
scarlet tails; they crouch
    over the smooth green
poles of its stalks like, yes,
    like dragonflies mating
clamped one on another,
    while ribbed leaves
like three-foot paddles
    stroke the artificial breeze.
But you'll have to imagine the scaly-
    breasted humming-bird
like a blur of purple-grey and
    viridian iridescence,
inserting the curve of its beak
    into the arc-ing corolla
like a key in the lock
    of its own front-door.

2. MADAGASCAR STAR ORCHID (*Angraecum sesquipedale*)

White giant of the rain-
    forest firmament
        you hang your pale

star high in the leaf
    canopy, reserving
        the foot-long spur

of your nectary for the lover
    Darwin foretold – the
        hawk-moth who

alone is able to recite
    your many-syllabled
        secret sweetness

on its long-imagined
    tongue: golden *xanthopan*
        morganii praedicta.

3. PITCHER-PLANT (*Nepenthes*)

Watch out for Aladdin's old brown slippers
whose curling toes dangle above your head.
Each droops on a boot-lace stalk
that grows from the very tip of a leaf
after the fruit has come and gone.
The small ones remind me
of wrinkled leather finger-stalls,
or withered condoms –
the ones the ancient Egyptians made
from sheep's intestine,
cotton or rice-paper,
rims fashionably rolled.
These pitchers are lethal pots,
nectaries that lure their prey –
insects, mostly – trapping them
in order to ingest a blow-fly,
midge or mosquito soup.
There is also one
that's large and patient enough
to cook up a broth of rats.

SWALLOWS

i. m. Mark Ogle

'Open, open the door to the swallow – '
GILBERT WHITE, after a carol by Athenæus

'I am open to an offer for this gem o' creation.'
The hay-trusser who will rise to be Mayor of Casterbridge
is selling his wife.
                    His words hang in the air
with the smell of furmity and trampled grass.
And at that moment
Hardy allows a swallow to enter the tent –
the home-loving swallow that mates for life;
that flies five thousand miles to build
year after year beneath the same eaves.
One of the last, she has lingered late this year
and flies *in quick curves* above their heads
until she finds a way out and is gone.
All have followed it with their eyes, silent,
tranced, and for a while it seems
the drunkard's words have been erased.
But soon, in spite of the bird, wife and child
are sold to a sailor and, like the swallow, gone.

*

Like your swifts, our swallows return mid-May –
earlier in recent years – but punctual
as the half-past-eleven wren that dots
and stutters round bins and tubs like a brown mouse.
Suddenly: one pair of swallows, then two, more;
hawking above the blossom in the garden.
You greet your swifts' return to that exact
window every year with joy and amazement:
travellers *extraordinaires*, who have flown
halfway round the earth, yet barely know it –

59

with vestigial feet, sleeping on the wing,
they inhabit the high air with their frenzied screams.
It has always meant bad luck to shut them out:
on the island of Rhodes when swallows arrived with spring
the children went 'a-swallowing' round the village
for figs, and wine, and wheat and cheese, chanting
'Open, open the door to the swallow!'

*

At Clonbur, Binn Shleibhe's morning fields
had trapped the sun in their glittering net.
And we – leaving open an upstairs window –
had trapped a swallow. Hands cupped round a warm
no-weight of feathers, I elbowed the Velux skyward,
stretched my arms out and, opening my fingers
saw a bird vanish into *a memory*
of fields.
          By day they wove invisible threads
around us where we lay on the grass, reading;
skimming so close they fanned the hairs on arm
or head. Yet every year they leave, give up
their claim to what they've known as home – the barn,
the rafters where my torch-beam found them
blinking beside the sleeping nest
with small bats flickering round.
When we left, migrating homewards,
the swallows' voices from the roof-ridge
were gathering up the threads of the day.

FAMILY GAMES

I don't remember the name of the game,
only how much it made us laugh –
my sister, our grandmother and me – tears
rolling down our cheeks, sprawled in the sun
on that pocket-handkerchief of lawn.

The cards were in a rusty toffee tin.
Grandma read us the story, making it up,
later, after the paper got lost, pausing,
now and then, to take a card
and hand it to one of us to read aloud:

"The bride, Miss Ethel Montclair, was marrying
her childhood sweetheart, Mr Cyril Lloyd,
who worked as a (turn up a card) *broom-handle.*
The bride looked radiant in a (turn up a card)
smelly old rabbit-skin, walking up the aisle
beside her father, elegant in his best (turn up
a card) *chamber-pot.* Her bridesmaid, Miss Nellie
Standish, carried her bouquet of roses and
(turn up a card) *something the cat brought in.*
There were nearly one hundred guests, including
(turn up 3 cards) *last week's fly-blown Sunday-joint,*
a pair of auntie's coms, and a bowler-hat..."

It was pure anarchy, and we hugged ourselves,
couldn't believe our luck. A far cry
from the games we played at home, the family
saga where, for no good reason, we woke
as (turn up a card) *bad, wicked girls,*
never learning the trick of how to be (turn up

a card) *seen and not heard;* where, in my round
National Health specs, I was always cast
as (turn up a card) *a clumsy clot;* and where,
after we'd run away from home
and been brought back, our mother chased us
round the kitchen-table, brandishing
(turn up a card) a *broom-handle.*

TORTOISES

For years I wondered why all the tortoises
abruptly vanished. When we moved to Marseille
we'd found a whole dynasty, trundling along
the irrigation-channels of our large garden:
a grandfather the size of a football,
two babies that lay in my ten year-old palm
like scaly half-crowns, and lots in between;
they were the stars in the garden's cast
of lizards, blue salamander, scorpions,
praying mantis, bull-frogs, hoopoes.

It was 1955; the "Club France-Grande Bretagne"
was still delivering monthly parcels of food
to old Resistance fighters like *Tonton Churchill*
in the mosquito-infested Camargue. Father
was still battling – but garden pests, like snails;
then, when his peas and beans began to sprout,
I found the last tortoise, picked it up and screamed
at the maggots writhing in the shell, hurling it
into the oleanders. Now I mourn them and him –
the guilty, bumbling casualties of war.

CUTTING MY FATHER'S HAIR

This morning, the birds' water-bowl
was frozen, coarse frost trapping
a few ragged scraps of down.
When I prised off the thick lid,
the underside was a bed of moss-
crystals, winter's ephemera;
a brash of ice-fronds, a fern-
forest astonishing in its beauty;
each fragile stem spatulate,
growing a lobe

as delicately rounded
as this that I must fold back
out of the way of my scissors.
Grey wisps of hair drift down
like the feathers of strange birds.
The rims of your ears
are frosty with eczema.
Towel around your shoulders
you sit, remote in your deafness;
shrouded like heavy furniture
in a cold, empty house.

STILL

after "Old Woman Cooking Eggs" *by Diego Velázquez*

Where does such stillness begin?
In the woman's tranced gesture—
the wooden spoon arrested, poised
above the terracotta dish, the egg
in her left hand never to be broken?
Or with the dreaming boy who has come
to a standstill here, encumbered with messages—
a flask of oil, a melon tied with string?

It seems a room where anything could happen,
each thing teetering on the edge of light:
a brass basin tenders its dented radiance;
an onion shimmers like a courtesan
in purple silk; the eggs in their glinting dish
are dithering; and the huge melon,
its skin scarred by earth, shines
as though the boy had taken a hempen lure
and gone out fishing to catch the moon.

MOON AND BLACKBIRD

Stopping above the park tonight
I watched the moon, just-risen, clear
the dark cape of the cedars, and sail
into a deep blue bay; and then the thought,
that surely it wasn't her but we ourselves
were moving? With that, earth reeled visibly
eastward and I was tottering and swaying.

I remembered the hen-blackbird
feeding earlier in the rowan, the branch
plunging and rising as she edged
down towards bright clustered berries;
how she had bounced and floundered
but kept her grip. With eyes shut
I held on to her brown feathers,
and was steadied, earthed.

Abandoned shieling among the broom,
the *borda* stands roofless, walls in a tumble;
raspberry canes thrive in an empty room.

Folk spent whole summers here beside their flocks,
where green hellebores flop like ghosts of dogs,
the mullein a grey wife by the gable.

There were never cushions until thyme
piled fragrance at the foot of walls
where brown saprophytes climb,
clawing the air like rusted tools.

Pale echo among the sheep bones,
sneezewort lingers,
and 'herb of hunger'
lifts its yellow face between stones.

SHEEP-BELLS IN THE PYRENEES

Someone has run to *La Bastida* to tell us,
"The sheep are coming! They're bringing the sheep
down from the hill!" We make for the back of the village,
to where the path winds up behind the pens
through meadows of poppies, scabious, pinks.
Far-off, a sound like water trickling
over stones, a pied, persistent music.
Two old shepherds, on their feet now,
shading their eyes, peering up the track
where a cloud of dust is snaking down,
white over grass, through poplars and broom,
the old men grinning as the flock comes into view.

Bleating, running full-tilt, skipping and leaping,
a torrent of sheep, recently shorn
to a deep-chested candour; with the brown ears
and panda-faces, brown muzzles and knees
of the *Ripollesa*, their smell eye-watering.
The heaviest bells are as big as a sheep's skull,
hammered iron, soldered and faced with tin,
quadrangular, with clappers of boxwood or bone;
they dangle from sturdy collars, carved from pine,
painted with daisies, zigzags, radiant suns,
to ward off the lightning of summer storms.

The sheep flow past in evening light,
their hooves clicking on stone; some plunder
the elder bushes or leap over the wall
to snatch a last green taste of orchard grass
before two scruffy sheepdogs chase them out;
a river of woolly bodies, their bells jangling,
commingling, like the peals of ten cathedrals

ringing out in a pandemonium
of sound and light and stink and dust.

Now, if I say their names out loud,
if I say

    borombes, trucs, cabroneres,
    picardes, andorranes, picarols,
    truquetes, trincoletes, esquellerincs,

something of that wild music returns
and I'm back on that low wall in Farrera, waiting.

A SHEPHERD'S VOICE

after two pictographic clay tablets from Tell Brak, Syria, c. 4000 BCE

The river the clay was dug from
has vanished, so we must imagine

ducks squabbling
among the rushes, the flight

of cranes at sunset, night
erupting with bull-frog cries.

What's scratched into the clay
is a voice, a shepherd's, who declares

– *Here are 10 goats*
– *Here are 10 sheep*

His dry receipts remain
to tell us that barren desert

was pasture, watered, green;
and though his flocks have shrunk

to two baked bits of clay,
what's scratched there is

the shepherd's voice, calling
his beasts into our field of vision –

some lop-eared with rough brown coats,
others whose big horns coil like rope:

– Here are 10 goats
– Here are 10 sheep

coming to drink, bells clunking, sending up
bird-cries; the reeds confer, the water laps.

FROM THE MUSICAL INSTRUMENT MUSEUM, BERLIN
especially a violin made by Jakob Stainer in 1654

A build-up of heat all week, and now
darkness accumulates above the Tiergarten.

A sprinkler flings, whirls, and flings its plume
over the dry lawns while, in my headphones,
Sol Babitz plays, on this very violin
in the display-case, the presto
from Bach's sonata in G minor.
Sol, Jakob, and Johann Sebastian
are playing an orchard:

bird's eye maple, pear, and walnut
rise and ramify in twigs of light;
arpeggios glitter with prefigured rain
and in the garden, thunder prowls
through patterns of lindenbloom and leaves;
in rainbow chords, those triple
or quadruple stops, wind bows the branches.

A man comes running out to tug the hose
inside. Sprinkler and violin die
as rain spots the stones then drums
on the glass roof *fortissimo*

.

SEDGE-WARBLERS ON THE MEON

i. m. Edward Thomas

Clear chalk-stream cadences
weave around stones,
combing the dark weed free.

On the bridge this spring
we follow the play
between river-bed and surface;

how the Meon's glitter is inflected
by deep notes of topaz flint,
braiding a path among the crowfoot;

yellow kingcup flowers open,
mouths like distant bugles calling
above the rush of water. And it's today

and a hundred years ago, this singing
of sedge-warblers, frantic, harsh
and shrill among the willows.

EVENING LIGHT

for Swithun and for Philip Levine

After taking our son to the station
we decide not to go straight home
but drive for a while, letting his calm presence
become the fields of evening,
his silent kindness linger in light
that casts long shadows on a road
we marched along when younger than he is now:
anxious students clutching our banner,
who feared for the window-poles
borrowed without permission, we
were marching against the war in Vietnam.
We were to have marched in silence,
but a small bunch of self-styled Maoists
kept up a chant of *Dien Bien Phu!*
As we crossed the bridge,
the Eden shrugged off our voices,
tossing them back at us diminished.
Impatient with the revolutionaries
I was a naïve girl wanting only to listen
to a curlew's melancholy calling, the voices
of oyster-catchers in the estuary; my thoughts
tumbling and wheeling like lapwings.
They were as common then as buzzards now.
Where have the lapwings gone? A buzzard
silently lifts from a gatepost as we pass
and merges with the screaming fighter
rising from the base and Iraq-bound.
The birds are different but the wars
are the same, only changing their names,
and we are still marching, ashamed

of what is being done in our name.
It was November then, and dark
when we shuffled into Cupar, the shops
all shut and no one around to take our leaflets.
At times it seems as though this is the most
we ever achieve: to march into darkness,
into silence, our words unheard
or blown about like litter. But sometimes
it is our children who redeem us,
lending their benevolent strength.
Hoisting tattered banners
we stumble onward with gifts all undeserved –
these fields of evening light
whose merciful shadows point us home.

THE CUPBOARD

for Claire Dubos

At this hour in Asnières,
the big burr-walnut cupboard

in the darkest corner of the hall
is waking up. Late afternoon sun,

low in the horse-chestnut tree
out in the windy garden, strikes

through the study-window
and begins to dance, waking the grain

so that the wood glows, comes alive
with hidden landscapes – hill-forts,

forest clearings, pools where trout
break the surface in rings of gold.

Every day of that week of silent skies,
all planes grounded by volcanic ash,

I watched the cupboard's hour-long
transformation, and was consoled.

DURA DEN FOSSIL FISH
Holoptychius andersoni

from the account given by the Rev John Anderson of Newburgh, 1859

Just as we were finishing
our grassy picnic – chicken-,
ham-, and pigeon-pies, peaches,
nectarines, apricots, plums
and grapes, all washed down
with draughts of cider, sherry –
there came a great shout: we ran,
some tumbling, falling over.
They had split a yellow sand-
stone slab, and lo! A great fish
lay at our astonished feet.
Briefly *a life-like glistering*
lingered on its scaly forms –
like a memory of light playing
upon a shrinking loch – then fled,
leaving dull, extraordinary stone.

THREE POEMS FOR NATASHA KANAPÉ FONTAINE

1. I Have Lost My Bearings

A fox barks and the door creaks
as though the wood
remembered the tree it once was.

I write this at a kitchen table
in the city, a plane passing
every minute, day and night.

It is time to go north. I want
to listen to silence and unpick its voices:
the wind that surges through pines

is only one of them, with the burn
that gurgles, chants, or roars in spate;
the buzzard mewing, wheeling overhead,

the oyster-catcher piping her way
across moorland, whisper of bog-cotton
surrendering to the wind. At Sanna

the machair will be bright with orchids.
Do you hear a humming, like fridge-song?
An emerald damsel-fly hovers above the burn.

2. TAKING ROOT

Now that the snows have gone
        and the beech unpleats
her tender green

in the woods of Druim na Drochaid
        I will go barefoot
                among the juicy stalks
shod in the *brog na cubhaig*
                the blue shoes the cuckoo wears

        a shade the flower
                barely assumes,
letting it float   like blue smoke

        a drift of light I wade through
                                under trees
        that spread their hands like a blessing

                In the woods of Druim na Drochaid
        among the twigs and leaf-mould
                my wandering feet
                        will finally
                        take root.

3. THE BRAIDED RIVER

The sun sets upriver
where my mother's folk
would row across each day
to work the forge at Albaston
and then row home: blacksmiths
from New Quay; fishermen,
smugglers and excisemen
of Mevagissey.

They hoisted the red sail at dawn
and at dusk lowered blue nets
with a catch of stars
that glittered like fish-scales.

Wise to every shoal and channel
their lives were woven
into the river's braid;
those who put out to sea
when the huer's cry of *Hevva!*
rang from the cliff-top, knew
as they watched the moon
bob among jellyfish
that at any moment
their life might unravel
into ribboning wrack.

SKELETON OF CHAMELEON
Chamaeleon chamaeleon

Clipped like a fountain-pen
to a glass stalk, as though to write

the bare bones of its life:
how Mulungu sent chameleon

to tell mankind, his new creation,
that they would never die.

But lazy chameleon loitered,
catching flies along the way with its long tongue.

Then envious lizard ran to earth
to tell mankind the contrary,

writing their fate in dust. If you happen
upon chameleon clinging to a twig

with clever claws and curling tail,
he will still blush and try

to hide himself
away.

based on a Bantu legend

FROM THE HINTERLAND

for Kazimierz Kuczynski, F.R.C.S. Edinburgh, and his wife, Alicia

This is a world turned inside-out,
a republic of the flesh
both strange and strangely familiar.

The walls are hung with oils,
portraits of common soldiers
who fought at Corunna or Waterloo,
where Charles Bell, army-surgeon,
paints the sun going down in musket-wounds,
with full colours, in a glory
that pale flesh puts on before nightfall.
Below, he adds medical notes, questions
treatment, fumes at his own helplessness.

The tables are laid with sprigged china, glass-ware,
entire canteens of polished cutlery:
here are tools for cutting and slicing,
for gripping and probing; even a saw.
But though the cabinets are replete
with choice cuts, the guests
departed years ago.

Some packed up and left, when bodies
grew into homes they couldn't call their own –
unnatural fruit sprouting from floorboards,
timbers shivering into Flemish lace.
As though flesh were determined
to enter the realm of metaphor,
blossoming and hardening
into mineral and vegetable forms
both beautiful and deadly –
one with Crohn's disease leaving
when her bowel became a draper's shop,

stuffed to the gills with pleated, peach-coloured satin;
others retreating as from a volcano
when X-rayed lungs threw up
carcinomas bright as agates;
when skin began to boil, to erupt
in melanomas black as basalt.

Still others groaned with the knowledge
of kidneys turned stone-quarries, sweating
to produce calculi of the finest limestone
and, now and then, a staghorn –
a rough, encrusted twelve-point antler;
a collector's item, having the shape
of the renal pelvic calyceal system.
We use lasers now to shatter kidney-stones,
but fragments may still clump in the ureter,
forming a *steinstrasse* – a cobbled street –
down which the surgeon ventures,
retrieving bits with a mere 'basket'.
Perhaps these ordinary names subdue
some ancient fear of having crossed
a threshold into forbidden places.

Little by little, the body gives up its secrets,
speaks back to us: is it an accident
the structure of the renal pelvis resembles
a calyx, that inner forms, as though to hint
at ancient kinship, should call up
the ghostly presences of plants?
Our nervous system branching, fanning out,
is sheathed like fennel, fine as asparagus-fern;
arteries, veins, capillaries ramifying
like algae, like rosy nets of *corallina*
left by the tide. Morphologies of flow,

like the child's plait the Amazon makes,
seen from the moon, map our dependence
on the laws of life; our kinship real,
in our shared need for water, air and light.

And who can doubt that water was once our home,
seeing these skeletons of fœtal hands,
these minute brown transparent bones
poised in jars of formalin?
Delicate as the bodies of insects,
articulated like marine crustaceae,
these are travellers from the hinterland
whose journey ended even before it began.
Fish-bones, writing their brief histories
in runes, in ogham-script the colour of blood;
whose perfect, counted fingers
make my own eyes swim with salt.

UNNAMED

It seems they've caught you at last
though we have only
the station-master's word for it.

Out of a forest of leopard and porcupine
you must have crept down to the cutting
at Haputale, its pines hung with vapour,
dripping ferns.

Bamboozled, were you,
by the fantastic arrangement
of plastic rone propped in a forked
twig to catch water running
cleanly off rock;
or by the other nifty set-up
of split bamboo and blue plastic
couched in lichen, mosses, valerian?

Smaller than
the smallest water-drop,
you're inching towards summer
when you'll be scrambling up
those final hairpin bends of rainforest,
your mission to re-arrange our lives;
persistent and serious
as that boy with a huge bunch
of crimson blossom
who shamed us into giving him
a hero's welcome.

I'm sending this early:
as you'll see,
it's written in pencil,
in case it turns out that the whole story
is only another of those dreams I keep having.

GLASS SPONGE: VENUS' FLOWER BASKET
Euplectella aspergillum

Some early Cambrian imperious gene has it constructing
a self in the very deepest, coldest ocean canyons, extracting

silica from water to put together an ice-palace,
six-pointed spicules shaping themselves into a dazzling cut-glass

vase, hollow, end-stopped, elegant, and flexible,
transmitting light better than any fibre-optic cable –

light drawn, deep in the absolute dark, from bio-luminescent
organisms, *living Lamps*, through a tuft of fibres, nascent

at the lens-shaped base, like an inverted crown. Become
a glowing beacon, the atrium attracts two home-

hunting shrimp – *spongicola* – who swim in through a gap
in the hexactinellid web and stay, feeding and cleaning a trap

they will grow too large to leave. In Japan, the sponge with resident
pair of shrimp is given as a traditional wedding-present.

DIVER

for Judy, i.m. Martin Dean

Because I knew you had dived, once,
in these waters, charting the *San Juan
de Sicilia*, and because I'd stand and scan,

early and late, our inlet for the otter,
your greater absence lingered
in the play of light on water:

as the tide dropped, bladder-wrack
dried in the sun, popping and cracking
like your outrageous jokes;

when the tide rose and flowed back in,
towing long cloaks of weed, puckering
the evening's golden skin,

a diver came on its own, plunging,
gone; then surfacing far off in a ring
of ripples, black throat tilted

at that precise and elegant angle,
before it erased itself in a single
question-mark, as someone called me in.

Grasspoint, Mull, August 2015

TREES DANCING

for the Canadian Zen artist, Chan Ky Yut

a tree holds early morning light
like another year
glittering with possibilities

nothing more silent
than the midnight evergreen
in which forty songbirds are roosting

when the sou'wester blows
and the sycamore threshes this way and that
how can we tell which of the two is singing?

the wild geese are passing
like twigs blown across the sky:
the oak's roots fasten more tightly on stone

on a mild day in winter
the box tree's scent reached after her
and she turned, thinking she heard her lover's voice

red and gold, leaves are falling
around the beech tree's foot, composing
a treatise on the beauty of nakedness

the myrtle's fingers, fanned against the blue;
the cherry tightly-sashed in satin; the painter
rising at dawn – all are part of the dance

CROW (CORVUS)

We meet on an eye-beam of mistrust –
glinting, licorice-black bead
and blue human iris – and I see
you know I know you know me,
the one at the window who flaps her arms
to drive you from the small birds' food.
But this time you hold your ground, hop
sideways, crouch, huddle, and gather
your oily, draggled skirts to fly but
not before grabbing a beakful of meal
with a wink to tell me you've
put one over me again, trickster,
dissembler, story-teller; I have read
how you stopped for figs, hungry
while fetching water for Apollo,
and how you made up some tale
about a snake at the spring; but even
bringing a snake in your claws
couldn't fool the god, and he hurled
you, cup and snake into the sky
where you glint at night, the cup
just out of reach of a thirsty bird.
I let you be, and turn away.
I'm not on the side of the gods.

ANNA CROWE was born in Plymouth, and educated in France and Sussex. She studied French and Spanish at the University of St Andrews where she now lives, working as a writer and translator. She has also been a primary school teacher, taught at the former Bede Monastery Museum in Jarrow, and worked for many years in the Quarto, the much-missed second-hand bookshop. She has tutored for the Open Association of St Andrews University and for the Open College of the Arts, and ran a poetry workshop for almost twenty years.

With others, in 1998 she founded StAnza, Scotland's Poetry Festival, was Artistic Director for the first seven years, and still serves as Honorary President on the Board of Trustees.

Her work includes two Peterloo collections, *Skating Out of the House* and *Punk with Dulcimer,* and three Mariscat chapbooks, *A Secret History of Rhubarb, Figure in a Landscape* (a PBS pamphlet Choice and winner of the Callum Macdonald Memorial Award) and *Finding My Grandparents in the Peloponnese.* She won the Peterloo Poetry Competition in 1993 and again in 1997, and has been a runner-up in the National Poetry Competition. She was awarded the Elmet Prize in 2018. Her work has been translated into Catalan, Spanish, German and Italian, including two of her collections: *Punk with Dulcimer* into Castilian by the Catalan poet, Joan Margarit, *Punk con salterio,* (Cosmopoética, 2008), and *Figure in a Landscape* into Catalan, as *Paisatge amb figura* (Ensiola, 2011), inspiring a series of lithographs by the Mallorcan sculptor, Andreu Maimó; and into Spanish by the Mexican poet, Pedro Serrano, and published in Mexico as *Figura en un paisaje* (El oro de los tigres 2018).

Books of translation include an anthology of Catalan poems, *Miralls d'aigua / Light off water,* a joint Carcanet / Scottish Poetry Library publication; work by the Catalan poet, Joan Margarit, *Tugs in the fog* (awarded a PBS Recommendation in 2006), *Strangely happy* and *Love is a Place* (all published by Bloodaxe); *Barcelona Amor Final:* anthology of poems about the city of Barcelona by Joan Margarit in Catalan, Castilian and English (Proa 2007); *No hi ha treva per a les fúries* (with Joan Margarit): translations into Catalan of poems by RS Thomas, (Proa 2013); *Six Catalan Poets, Peatlands*, poems by the Mexican poet, Pedro Serrano, and *Lunarium*, poems by the Mallorcan poet, Josep Lluís Aguiló (all published in parallel text by Arc). Her translations of the work of the Catalan poet, Manuel Forcano, *Maps of Desire*, is forthcoming from Arc in 2019. In 2006 she received a Travelling Scholarship from the Society of Authors, to further her work of translation.

She enjoys collaborating with professionals in other disciplines – painters, sculptors, textile artists, jewellers and calligraphers. Her poetry has been recorded for the Poetry Archive and is available at www.poetryarchive.org One of the things that drives her need to write is the desire to rescue obscure stories and give a voice to things that might otherwise have no voice and be forgotten or overlooked.

She lives in St Andrews with her partner, Dr Julian Crowe. They have three grown-up children and five grandchildren.

www.ingramcontent.com/pod-product-compliance
Lightning Source LLC
LaVergne TN
LVHW041233080426
835508LV00011B/1186